# HUGELY HILARIOUS JOKES ABOUT DINOSAURS

Julia Garstecki

BLACK
RABBIT
BOOKS

Hi Jinx is published by Black Rabbit Books
P.O. Box 227, Mankato, Minnesota, 56002.
www.blackrabbitbooks.com
Copyright © 2022 Black Rabbit Books

Marysa Storm, editor; Michael Sellner, designer
and photo researcher

Library of Congress Cataloging-in-Publication Data
Names: Garstecki, Julia, author.
Title: Hugely hilarious jokes about dinosaurs /
by Julia Garstecki.
Description: Mankato, Minnesota : Black Rabbit Books,
[2022] | Series: Hi jinx. Just for laughs |
Includes bibliographical references and index. |
Audience: Ages: 8-12 | Audience: Grades: 4-6 |
Summary: "Through an engaging design that brings the
jokes to life with fun facts and critical thinking questions,
Hugely Hilarious Jokes about Dinosaurs will have readers
laughing and learning"– Provided by publisher.
Identifiers: LCCN 2020016595 (print) | LCCN 2020016596
(ebook) | ISBN 9781623107055 (hardcover) |
ISBN 9781644665602 (paperback) | ISBN 9781623107116 (ebook)
Subjects: LCSH: Dinosaurs–Juvenile humor. | Dinosaurs–
Juvenile literature.
Classification: LCC PN6231.D65 G37 2020 (print) |
LCC PN6231.D65 (ebook) | DDC 818/.602–dc23
LC record available at https://lccn.loc.gov/2020016595
LC ebook record available at https://lccn.loc.gov/2020016596

## Image Credits

# CONTENTS

# Chapter 1

# Let's Get Laughing

Scientists have named about 1,000 different dinosaurs. Who knows how many we have yet to discover? Scientists continue to search for more new dinosaurs all around the world. While they search, you can read on to unearth some dinosaur jokes. Use them to make your family and friends roar with laughter.

# Chapter 2
# Jokes aBout Dino SPorts

Why was the Stegosaurus such a
good volleyball player?

*Because it could really spike the ball.*

## Fun Fact

William G. Morgan invented volleyball in 1895.
Dinosaurs didn't get the chance to play. They
died out about 64 million years before that.

What do you call a dinosaur
that hates to lose?

*a saur-loser*

What do you
get when a
dinosaur makes
a touchdown?

*a dino-score*

How did the dinosaur feel
after lifting weights?
*pretty dino-sore*

What do you get when dinosaurs have a **demolition derby**?

*Tyrannosaurus wrecks*

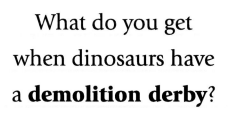

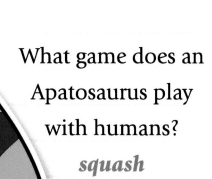

What game does an Apatosaurus play with humans?

*squash*

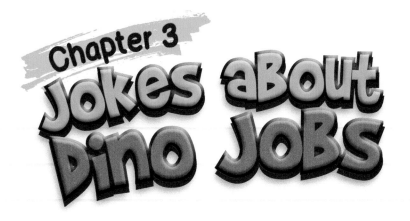

# Chapter 3
# Jokes about Dino Jobs

What do you call a dinosaur

that works as a magician?

*a dino-sorcerer*

What do you call a dinosaur
that works on a ranch?

*Tyrannosaurus Tex*

Which dinosaurs were
police officers?

*Tricera-cops*

12

Where do meat-eating dinosaurs work as clowns?

*At the **carnivore**.*

What do dinosaur butchers use to make sausage?

*Jurassic pork*

# Chapter 4

# Jokes aBout Dino Pastimes and More

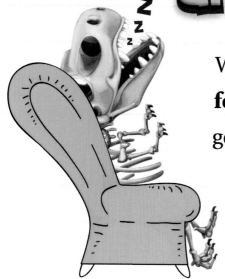

What do you call **fossils** that don't get off the couch?

*lazy bones*

What do you call a dinosaur fart?

*A blast from the past.*

Let me tell you about a dinosaur that only eats plants. You've probably never heard of **herbivore**.

## Fun Fact

Some foods, such as beans and broccoli, make you fart more. Some dinosaurs ate plants. Others ate meat. Some ate both. We're not sure if their food made the dinos fart, though.

What did the dinosaur say when it saw the volcano explode?

*What a lavaly day!*

**Fun Fact**
Some scientists believe a giant volcanic eruption wiped out the dinosaurs.

Why did dinosaurs
eat raw meat?
*Because fire wasn't
invented yet.*

Why did the dinosaur
go to the disco?
*Because it was a
disco-saurus.*

What do you call a
sleeping dinosaur?
*a dino-snore*

What do you call
a polite dinosaur?
*a please-yosaur*

Why didn't the dinosaur cross the road?

*Because there weren't any.*

What kind of burger can a herbivore eat?

*a trees-burger*

# Chapter 5
## Get in on the Hi Jinx

Paleontologists study dinosaurs. They dig up fossils and use technology, such as **X-rays**, to learn about them. They figure out how old the fossils are. They examine teeth shape to see if the dinosaur was a meat or plant eater. If you enjoyed this book's jokes, you might want to be a paleontologist when you grow up. Until then, you can use their discoveries to make new dinosaur jokes!

# Take It One Step More

1. Do you think you'd like a job as a paleontologist? Why or why not?

2. Pick your favorite joke from the book. What makes it so funny? Write a similar joke.

3. What is your favorite dinosaur? Can you write a joke about it?

# GLOSSARY

**carnivore** (KAR-nuh-vor)—a meat-eating animal

**demolition derby** (dem-uh-LISH-uhn DUR-bee)—a contest in which drivers in old cars crash into each other until only one car is still running

**eruption** (ih-RUHP-shuhn)—a sudden explosion

**fossil** (FAH-sul)—the remains or traces of plants and animals that are preserved as rock

**herbivore** (HERB-uh-vor)—a plant-eating animal

**squash** (SKWOSH)—a game played in a four-wall court with a long-handled racket and a rubber ball that can be hit off any number of walls; it also means to beat or press into a soft or flat mass.

**X-ray** (EKS-rey)—powerful, invisible rays that can pass through objects and make it possible to see inside things

## BOOKS

**Daniels, Patricia.** *1,000 Facts about Dinosaurs, Fossils, and Prehistoric Life.* 1,000 Facts About. Washington, D.C.: National Geographic Kids, 2020.

**Rusick, Jessica.** *World's Best (and Worst) Gross Jokes.* Laugh Your Socks Off! Minneapolis: Lerner Publications, 2020.

**Taylor, Charlotte.** *Digging Up Dinosaur Fossils.* Digging Deep into Fossils. New York: Enslow Publishing, 2022.

## WEBSITES

Dino Road Trip
**kids.nationalgeographic.com/videos/dino-road-trip/**

Dinosaur Facts
**www.dkfindout.com/us/dinosaurs-and-prehistoric-life/dinosaurs/**

Jokes for Kids: Big List of Dinosaur Jokes
**www.ducksters.com/jokes/
dinosaurs.php**